Learning from home-based education

An Education Now Special Report

edited by

Roland Meighan

Education Now Books

First published 1992
by Education Now Publishing Co-operative Ltd
(Office: 113 Arundel Drive, Bramcote Hills, Nottingham NG9 3FQ)

Reprinted 1998 and 2000

British Cataloguing in Publication Data

British Library Cataloguing in Publication Data

Learning from Home-based Education

    I. Meighan, Roland
    371.103

ISBN   1-871526-06-X

Design and production: Education Now Books

Reprinted by Esparto Digital Ltd., Derby

Contents

Never too late, to learn to educate

by Roland Meighan

In the UK. and the U.S.A. and in various other countries an unusual, quiet revolution has been taking place in the form of educating children at home. At the same time as the fierce debates about mainstream education have been taking place concerning the National Curriculum, Testing, 'Back to the Basics', Opting Out or Opting In, Local Management of Schools, etc., some families have just quietly been getting on with a 'Do It Yourself' approach to education. In the U.S.A. over a million families are now 'home-schoolers' as they are known across the Atlantic. In the UK. over 10,000 families are estimated to be operating home-based education.

This phenomenon is more accurately described as home-based education because the majority of families use the home as a springboard into a range of community-based activities and investigations rather than try to copy the 'day prison' model of the local school. People find this quite hard to grasp and this is shown in the asking of questions about whether such children become social isolates. After a little thought, it is clear that learning activities out and about in the community give children more social contacts and more varied encounters than the restricted social life of a standard school, as well as breaking the peer dependency feature of adolescent experience in the 'day prison'.

Most people have come to believe that schooling is compulsory and are often taken aback to find that they are quite wrong. The families concerned get rather tired of quoting the law on the matter to correct this myth. Section 36 of the 1944 Education Act (England and Wales) states that :

"It shall be the duty of the parent of every child of compulsory school age to cause him to receive efficient full-time education suitable to his age, aptitude and ability, either by regular attendance at school or otherwise."

The law is clear, education is compulsory, schooling is not. This is one of many examples where common sense and common information is at odds with the facts.

Education Otherwise

In 1976 a self-help and mutual support organisation was set up for parents in the UK. who choose this unusual form of education: it took its name from the clause in the Education Act and was therefore entitled *Education Otherwise*. When I began to research into this development there were about twenty families involved. Now there are at least four thousand, including those who are not associated with the organisation *Education Otherwise*.

Does it work?

There are several kinds of answer to the question of 'how effective is home-based education?'

(a) Reference can be made to the achievements of people educated this way. Some are well known people, some living, some dead, such as Yehudi Menuhin, Patrick Moore, Agatha Christie, Margaret Mead, Thomas Edison, George Bernard Shaw, Noel Coward, C.S.Lewis, Pearl Buck, Bertrand Russell, John Stuart Mill. I have also encountered a number of less famous but publicly prominent people such as Harry Stopes-Roe, the philosopher of science, and Sheila Wright, ironically the former chair of Birmingham Education Committee and former MP. for Handsworth. There are many more.

(b) Reference can be made to current academic successes gained by home-based students e.g. Sarah Guthrie's daughter admitted to York University, the Everdell's son admitted to Cambridge, and the Lawrence's daughter admitted to Oxford aged 13.

(c) Reference can be made to the World-wide Education Service (WES) of the Parents National Education Union founded by Charlotte Mason. WES have been educating children at home both in the UK. and abroad for over a hundred years by means of a correspondence course for the parents using similar principles of distance teaching to those of the Open University.

(d) Reference can be made to the court case Harrison v. Stevenson, that led to the judge concluding that:

"We are satisfied that for these children, their manner of education has proved efficient. They are mature, confident and at ease in all sorts of company. They are lively minded, have a good general knowledge and are intellectually athletic ... In their case their education - in its own field - has proved and is proving, a marked success."

'In its own field' meant that the Harrison family had elected for autonomous education based on practical and self-sufficiency skills rather than an academic approach.

(e) In my research at least three different kinds of home-based education have been identified:

i. Parents who want an academic form of education for their children and decide that they can they can achieve this better at home than at school.

ii Parents who have unhappy or unsuccessful children at school and decide to improve things by home-based education. They have always been successful in effecting such an improvement in the hundreds of cases I have seen.

iii Parents who want a different form of education e.g. autonomous, self-directed learning or self-sufficiency skills, and know that schools do not provide it so they will have to do it themselves. The Harrison family, quoted above, fought out their right to do this in a prolonged court case.

Home-based education has been shown to work in all three categories.

(f) Another kind of response can be made to the imagined objections to home-based education e.g. lack of social life, difficulty with games, or science experiments etc. They prove, for the most part, to be imaginary because parents who adopt home-based education become resourceful in solving such problems. In the case of social behaviour, they find that their children usually become more skilled than schooled children, who tend to become increasingly peer-group dependent.

(g) Another source of reference is that of the presence in the ranks of the home-based educators of so many members of the teaching profession - at least 25% of the cases at any given time, and currently about 33% in the UK. - who have decided, with 'insider knowlege', that home-based education provides the best option for their own children.

Of course, it must be possible for home-based education to be a failure, but I just have not come across any cases. Some telling words come from one of the learners:

Dear Education Otherwise,

My best friend is Susan and she doesn't go to school; she is taught at home by her parents and is more interesting than someone that does go to school because she knows a lot more.

I sometimes feel a bit jealous of her, because she is more educated than some of my other friends and myself. At school there are quite a few bullies, but Susan doesn't have to worry about things like that. Sometimes I wish I was educated at home as well as Susan and her brother, Paul, as they can spend more time with their parents and pets.

At school, you hardly use a computer, but Susan and Paul nearly always use a computer and are shown how to use one properly. They are always learning about new things - at school I always learn about the same things over and over again!

Some teachers are hard to get on with and you don't get any encouragement from them, but your parents always give you encouragement.

Carol Ann, aged 12, from Bolton

Lessons I have learned from home-based education

Researching home-based education has been a remarkable experience that has helped me review most of my assumptions as a practising teacher about educational matters. I have come to feel very privileged to have been a witness to it all. Some of my personal conclusions are as follows:

1. Diversity in education is likely to be healthy
   - because individuals differ and families differ
   - because circumstances are different
   - because successful education can take many forms.
   (Therefore *always* suspect regimental 'answers' - such as the 'answer' of a British National Curriculum, or 'salvation by phonics', or 'salvation by testing'.)

2. Wounds can heal - children can recover from bad learning experiences especially in the supportive environment of a concerned family.

3. It is actually hard for a school to match an alert, organised and energetic family. Only a few schools even get near it.

4. Flexible learning, (and as a result the production of flexible people) is currently more likely to be found in home-based education.

5. Learner-managed learning (autonomous education) is more frequently found in home-based education: school tends to focus down on how to be taught

whereas homes tend to teach how to learn. (Schools tend to teach you to be stuck with the gaps in your knowledge, homes how to fill them.)

6. Confidence-building is more likely to be found in homes.

7. Non-sexist education can be achieved more easily at home.

8. The habit of peer-dependency can be broken by home-based education and the 'tyranny of the peer group' reduced.

9. The rotation and alternation of a variety of types of curriculum is commonplace at home, much rarer at school.

10. Schools tend to focus down on one-dimensional education, habituating their inmates to heavier and heavier doses of authoritarian forms of learning and behaviour patterns. Homes more frequently develop multi-dimensional education, alternating authoritarian with autonomous and with democratic forms of learning and behaviour. Thus, schools with their eventual rigid patterns of behaviour, after a more promising start in early childhood settings, tend to produce rigid people, whereas homes, with their more varied and fluid patterns, tend to produce more flexible and adaptable people. I will leave readers to judge which is more appropriate in the modern world, and which is the dinosaur option.

11. Co-operative and democratic forms of education are more likely to be found in home-based settings.

12. So-called 'school phobia' is actually more likely to be a sign of mental health, signalling the rejection of a continuous negative human experience, whereas the herd mentality of school dependency is a largely unrecognised mental health problem.

13. Homes are more likely than schools to achieve 'The child in pursuit of knowledge and not knowledge in pursuit of the child'. (George Bernard Shaw)

14 A positive way forward for the schooling system is to take up the idea favoured by many home-based educators of flexischooling. Some schools, especially Nursery Schools and some Infants Schools, are already experienced in the flexi-time, flexi-learning roles, and flexi-parental roles, that this requires.

15. It is never too late to learn to educate!

Instead of writing my own conclusion, I have decided to quote part of a letter from the Education Otherwise Newsletter number 82, October 1991, since it captures the spirit of what I have been trying to say:

"I would like to say how much I agree with Chris Shute's article ... Chris's comments about children behaving like shell-shocked Tommies when released from the mental straight-jacket of daily lessons was never more true than in my own case. After eleven years of fear/boredom caused by most of the teaching staff, and ducking and weaving from the mean-spirited pupils, I finally left school with no self-esteem, almost no confidence, and no interest in education whatsoever. I have spent the last twenty years in a state of suspended animation as far as having any particular interests for myself - that is - until very recently.

After a dear friend told me about EO five years ago I grasped it, and with my husband's backing decided to 'teach' our two boys from home. This was the first real initiative I had taken in years. I have found that as I have been 'teaching' the boys (for want of a better word) I too have also been learning. OK, so I am a late starter, perhaps slow even. But, guess what? I'm gradually beginning to get concerned about things again. I am about to take up some college courses that interest ME for my personal pleasure and satisfaction.

Passing examinations aren't the prime thing. The fact that the interest is coming back, and that I am now confident enough to try is a breakthrough in itself. I am almost recuperated. At last there is light at the end of the tunnel."

J.Nelson, Tamworth, Staffordshire

Starting out

(Thoughts on home education from the Trafford family)

Katherine (mother):

"Go for it!"
"I'm sure it would be right for the children, but what about you?"
"... and what about Technology?"
"How will you do the SATs?"
"I'm sure your children will become very independent and articulate."
*"I suppose it must be easier now that there is a National Curriculum
to follow."*
"Good luck; I wish I'd done it with mine."

These were some of the comments made to me by friends and colleagues during our deliberations over home education and 'going public' in the early summer of 1991. Whilst our two girls, Eleanor (seven) and Rachel (five and a half) were happy and doing well at school, we, as parents were not satisfied with what was on offer. So I resigned from my part-time job as a peripatetic music teacher and became a full-time home educator. We took government advice about the 'system' and opted out, but not in the way intended by the Tories, from LEA control. We went one step further, and have opted out of government interference in our children's education. The LEA maintains its responsibility by inspecting us regularly, but that is all. What we do, and how we do it, is now basically down to us. During the anxious spring of 1991, that seemed a heavy burden, but in reality it is not.

It is not a heavy burden because I am confident that I know what my children need now. They need challenges, and they need to extend their imaginations: where are these needs addressed in the hierarchical National Curriculum? I think that I have set myself difficult tasks, but at least I am making an attempt at them. I don't believe those two (to me) basic tasks were even identified in school. My hope is to guide the children's development, whilst at the same time maintaining breadth and balance, and to encourage their particular enthusiasms.

So we operate a 'flexible routine' at home, with no set timetable other than fixed activities such as dancing classes and gymnastics club. Where I have needed ideas or guidance in a particular area, I have usually found books to help; there are many available in shops and libraries, so there are no worries about resources. In aiming to develop every area of their education, the biggest problem has been finding time to do it all! I sincerely believe that children need to have as many different opportunities/experiences in their early years as possible. How else will they be able to make informed choices later on?

Yet there has emerged an imbalance in their lives, for which I make no apology and can only hope for it to continue! It is music (not exactly top priority in government circles). Both Eleanor and Rachel play the piano (learning from me on a 'need-to-know' basis), the violin (in a weekly, individual Suzuki lesson) and the recorder (descant and treble, playing solos, duets and trios). On average, we probably spend two hours a day on music-playing, singing and listening. The consequence is a vast musical education - intellectual, aesthetic and social. To me, these are the qualities which quite naturally spill over into other aspects of life and learning, with obvious advantages.

So where are we now? How far have we come? How far shall we go? These are often the questions of doubters, those who seek to compare (dare I say test?), even those who may be envious in some way. But they are valid questions which I find amusing to answer. First, at home we are in a very democratic and liberal 'learning environment', where we all have imput and responsibility. Second, we have ventured further and wider in the first six weeks than I thought possible. Third, we shall go as far as we can to the satisfaction of us all. After all, the four of us made that fateful decision in the early summer of 1991, and I hope that through experience and discussion we can all continue to make decisions and take responsibility for them, independent of government ideology.

Eleanor, aged 7:

I like learning at home because we don't have to write pages and pages of the same work. And I like going to dancing when we are not in a hurry from school to Daddy's school to get changed and eat our honey sandwiches. I like going swimming because I like pushing off from the side or end of the pool. I like watching the television. I have got a file full of work. I have got time to do my violin, piano and recorder practice. I like helping Mummy make cakes. Mummy is a good teacher.

Rachel, aged 5:

I like learning at home because I like going swimming because I like swimming on my back. And I like going dancing on Mondays. And I like watching Television. At the moment, we've watched Stop, Look, Listen and Music Time. I like playing on my bike. And Mummy and Daddy said they might buy me a new bike for my birthday. And I like helping Mummy bake cakes and bake the bread. I didn't like going to school because the playground was too noisy. At home I have a file full of work. When we were at school we had to squeeze in violin practice, piano practice, recorder practice and treble practice. Mummy is a good teacher. This is an article about learning at home. I am 5. Rachel Trafford

Bernard (father):

It is a bit of a cheek that I am writing about educating Eleanor and Rachel at home, because I do very little of it. On the other hand, as headmaster of a selective independent day school, I am perhaps asked more questions about our decisions and plans relating to home education than Katherine is, and gain more reactions from colleagues and acquaintances.

The first reaction in generally one of horror, quickly masked and turned into a polite observation, *"You are brave!"* I think they picture us in a running battle with the law (they tend to be as ill-informed about our rights as we used to be) and also to have a vision of recalcitrant children fighting and bickering as they often do at the end of a long summer holiday. Neither has proved to be the case. The local authority's inspectors in Wolverhampton have been charming and supportive, according to Katherine and the children, and we expect them to be de-registered without trouble in a few months.

We have always counted ourselves lucky that Eleanor and Rachel get on well and love doing things together. I do not claim and parental credit for that: it has just happened, but it undoubtedly helped us to make our decision, since we had few fears of constant arguments or sibling rivalry. I always come home from work to a happy household. Life is fulfilling for all of us: Eleanor and Rachel always have something that they are in the middle of, so we hardly ever hear that grumpy complaint, *"I'm bored."* They are always playing the violin, the piano or the recorder, writing or reading something, constantly doing and achieving things because they are so highly motivated, self-motivated, confident, even-tempered and fulfilled - I cannot overstate the sense of fulfilment that pervades the family. When I get home from work, there is work to see, experiments to witness, new tunes to hear, tales of expeditions, excitement and funny occurrences to be told. I think I am the only one of the family with regrets, and real sorrow, for my time-consuming job makes me miss so much of the fun.

Having heard me describe that state of affairs, the questioner generally falls silent. That is understandable. If home education is so wonderful, why isn't everyone doing it? And there is the underlying unease that there is something heretical or anti-social about it: after all, we all went through proper school, for better or worse. So I am usually prevented from going on to describe the effect that teaching Eleanor and Rachel at home has had on me as an educator.

Some close friends were very concerned that our home education plan might be used as a stick to beat me with professionally: how, after all, can a head openly support something which is 'anti-school'? I have not yet heard any such a criticism expressed. Like the head of the children's school, everyone with whom I have discussed our plans for home education seems to understand our genuinely held belief that we can do something better for our particular children at this particular time, and that we have nothing against schools and schooling - apart from the increasing political control we are witnessing. No-one has yet accused me, or any of us, of trying to undermine 'the system', whatever their private reservations may be.

I find myself now regarding methods of education as a continuum. At the one end there is the technique of a teacher expert lecturing to serried ranks of pupils who all work on exactly the same thing at precisely the same time. At the other end lies totally individualised and pupil-centred learning, the teacher acting as a consultant and adviser. The mode of education which a school tries to provide or which a parent chooses lies somewhere along that continuum, and there are inevitably compromises to be made and, one hopes, a variety of styles which may be adopted. The popular image of my independent ex-grammar school may well be one of 'serried ranks', but we are constantly making compromises between the cost-effectiveness of classes of 25 pupils and the need for individualisation and individuality in learning and achievement.

Katherine's and my vision of home education is, of course, very much at the 'individualised' end of the continuum. The lessons I am learning from Eleanor and Rachel are, however, profound: many preconceptions are being challenged and I am doing a great amount of radical thinking. I think that I am becoming a better head. Observing and helping Katherine, Eleanor and Rachel as they work together is informing all my attempts to encourage self-determination, individuality, creativity and democratic practice in every aspect of the school for which I am responsible, and Eleanor and Rachel are already living proof of the benefits of individualised and negotiated learning. Home education is good for the children: for the parents it is simply 'mind blowing', and for all of us, it is great fun.

Deschooling is not just for children

by Sue Pattullo

Three years ago it finally began to dawn on us with ominous clarity that it was not just going to be some far off secondary education we might eventually take issue with, but here and now, with primary education.

In whose best interests?

In the mid 1970's I had rejected a conventional university education halfway through. I finished my degree with an Amerian Quaker College, an apprentice-ship-based, learner-directed programme offering the whole world as its study ground. My ideas about education were shaped by that experience. When our son started school at 4, new parents were warned their children might turn into little monsters for the next few months. It was true, but why ever were we putting them through this? In the 1980's I was deeply involved with child care issues, especially as a Guardian Ad Litem, an independent person representing the child's needs in certain court proceedings, with a legal duty to present the child's views. 'In whose best interests?' was a question I now found myself asking in terms of schooling as well as welfare,

No answers

By chance I met up again with one of the pioneering head teachers from the 1970's. Sadly, the vision had been wrung out of him in the last 10 years. I met with a small group of people also dissatisfied with what was on offer in local schools to see if we could create a viable alternative. They devised a curriculum. I felt very uneasy about this development and withdrew. I visited four of the current pioneering schools and returned with more questions than answers.

Yes but

For a complexity of reasons our son finally came out of school 18 months ago, aged 6, and it was not just him who had to get school out of his system. The whole family began a process of deschooling. When opting into schooling you choose the best from what is on offer. When you home educate, the world is your oyster - you do it your own way. If you firmly believe that the three R 's should be practised daily, or believe in total freedom, then you are half-way to knowing how to proceed. We had no model The dilemmas, the 'yes buts', carried over from the 'shall-we-shan't-we-take-him out of school?' into the 'well-what-now-and-how?' At gut level we believed in a number of things but reconciling them in practice with all the ingrained and often conflicting running commentary emanating from our heads was a different matter.

We believed children's lives need to be integrated - an interweaving of emotional and intellectual and spiritual growth. But how integrated were we? How much were our own lives split up into non-interrelating segments? Was it fair/realisic/appropriate to attempt to avoid distinction between work and play?

We believed children need childhoods, to be able to grow up at their own pace, to play and fantasise. We believed they need to be protected from experiences they cannot as yet cope with and from unnecessary peer group pressure. We believed they should be listened to. But was it. O.K. for him to play in the sandpit for days on end? Would he learn to cope with nastiness and bullying if not bullied young?

We believed in the idea of self-directed learning but would he miss some vital 'building block' or wonderful opportunity - his right from the National Curriculum? Would he blame us later for not insisting on knowing what is best for him and applying pressure to stick at certain more tedious or difficult activities? What do we do when he refuses to show self motivation towards anything resembling maths?

What about the days when we get back from taking the cat to the vet, making the painter a cup of tea, answering 3 phone calls and going to tell the neighbour her dog has escaped? Somehow the morning has gone and 'nothing' has been done. Afternoons are never the same and anyway I am not so good at responding creatively to a request to help make kites at 5 p.m.

Slowly solutions evolve. In the morning we work together to get the house jobs done. We can then settle to his list of how he wants to spend his time - which gives me some sense of what is to come. I provide resources, offer extensions, ideas and trips, but I feel less need to orchestrate his education or clockwatch. In the morning, I am 'available' to help, in the afternoons - don't guarantee to be. Problems, such as maths and recorder practice, are discussed and we attempt to reach a consensus. And I no longer feel routine car journeys have to be made educational.

Deschooling us

We are now closer to understanding what self-directed education might mean in practice for our son (and younger daughter). We have also understood something else. Looking back, we realise that dissenting from something as large as the education system also meant dissenting from a large number of values that most of society accept more easily than we do. Taking a .stand in this area of our life has had a knock-on effect in other areas It has created questions, problems, unease and vulnerability. It has also created delight, excitement, wonder, satisfaction. It has started a whole chain of re-evaluation and critical examination of wider issues. It has opened the way for new ventures, new explorations, discoveries, challenges, knowledge, new skills, new feelings, new thoughts and a new sense of congruence. We have realised it is not just our children who are being educated. I have always liked Paulo Freire's definition of education as a process of *"becoming critically aware of one's reality in a manner which leads to effective action upon it"*. That is just what we have **all** been doing, and continue to do. We wonder why it took us so long!

A delightful happening:
Our experience of home-based education

by Roger and Tina Rich-Smith

Meet the children

We have three daughters: Emma, Samantha and Lucy-Anne (aged 11, 9, and 3 respectively). Emma and Samantha attended school until 1989.

Leaving school

The decision to withdraw our children from school was made in 1989. It was based on long term developments and feelings. We did not act on a sudden impulse or over-react to an isolated issue or upset. There were some matters that proved to be the last straw, but these merely reinforced the thinking we had already done.

Reasons for leaving

These were many and varied. The following came to dominate our perceptions of schools:

1. Ineffective at providing a 'suitable environment for young people'. Under this heading you could include everything from poor buildings and layout of classrooms, to distractions from disruptive pupils, poor teaching styles, and physical intimidation and mental intimidation. (Of course, we freely acknowledge that for many pupils school may also be a safer and better place to be than their home - and what that implies is another debate entirely!)

For us, though, two criteria came to dominate on this area. One was the inordinate and unhealthy influence of peer group pressure. And the other was the lack of any real moral and spiritual base to the educational proceedings. Christian teaching and moral character seem to be hung round the neck of a materialistic and self-centred educational giant like some hand-me-down talisman. This was not a situation that we agreed with or wanted for our daughters.

2. Ineffective at 'educating'! At the end of the day what is our educational system turning out? Our feelings were that the system was actually dysfunctional in respect of effective learning. Many of the structures, postures and administrative processes involved in modern education act against effective learning. Children become demotivated and merely perform for the teacher rather than become increasingly enthusiastic and alive with a spirit of adventure and sense of discovery. That precious attitude of 'wanting to find out' and explore possibilities seems so often to be replaced by an insidious lethargy. The *mechanics* of educating are there - teachers, schools and facilities - but the dynamics of effective and enjoyable learning are often missing - in spirit and in deed.

What price pupil interest and motivation when all those golden (and unique) 'first-time' learning situations in a young person's life are so often trodden by rigid timetables. Thus, and in other ways, is an understanding of the psychology of effective learning repeatedly thrown out of the window by the organisational expedient of the very system claiming to be best at educating.

We could, of course, elaborate on a number of specific issues (each a debate in itself) but sufficient now to say that, as parents, we were increasingly concerned that the environment, personnel and content (curriculum) of our daughters' education were largely outside our influence. Our conclusion was that home-based education would re-dress many of these problems.

Response from the Local Education Authority

Once the decision to remove our daughters from school had been taken, there was, of course, the matter of informing both the school and the LEA. We were not at all worried. Correspondence with other people who had experience of educating 'other than by attendance at school' also provided us with valuable insights into possible responses from the Authority.

We had run our own small pilot project of working at home during a vacation. This gave us limited but very clear ideas of what could be achieved and how the girls would actually work and respond to the new situation.

The school's response was the most hostile: an Education Welfare Officer (EWO) was sent round having been given inaccurate (or misleading?) information by the head. The EWO was sent away, never to return, and we followed the matter up with a firm letter. The LEA responded in a more professional manner and discharged their legal duty by arranging, and then sending, a senior inspector to visit. We tape-recorded the meeting, just in case there were problems. No hard offers of information or support were made, and no further communications were forthcoming.

Educating at home - a delightful experience

Having our daughters at home and taking responsibility for their education, has proved to be a delightful experience for us all. They do more work in half the time. There is less stress and, so far, no days off with any 'illness'. The girls have shown themselves keen to learn, hard-working and a joy to have about the place. They seem to be as committed to the idea of home-based education as we are - we would not have withdrawn them if they had wanted to remain at school. The extra work involved for us all is well worth the effort.

Education, or learning, should be an enjoyable experience. We try not to 'teach' our daughters. Rather the aim is to 'learn with them' - to encourage, support, guide, stimulate, enthuse and provoke interest.

School, of course, would claim to do just the same, only better because of their resources and expertise. Our experience, and we speak as teachers ourselves with many years of experience in a variety of educational environments, is that the opposite is more often the case. Little of that expertise is available per unit child - even if the teacher is good. As for the school resources, what is available anyway? How often is it used? How up-to-date are they? Are they really useful or necessary? Once you really start probing at the educational colossus, it rapidly falls apart.

We will not get involved in the debate about 'what is education anyway?' except to say that in our mind 'education' (or good education) has little to do with the artificial, bureaucratic and regimented environment of most schools.

What do we do then?

Our current situation may be described as fairly conservative: Roger works full-time in education and Tina organises the home and manages the day to day education programme of our daughters. Our approach is one of partnership. We may both have areas of defined skills and responsibilities, but all decisions about our daughters' learning are taken jointly. We also involve our daughters in those decisions rather than imposing on them a programme of study or subject they have little interest or enthusiasm for. Emma and Samantha currently do five mornings a week, Monday to Friday, of what might loosely be termed academic subject work. All afternoons are devoted to artistic, creative

mings only - academic work 17 -
noon - music + art - sport.

and physical pursuits. No work is given in the evening as we consider this time of day should be reserved for family activities, outside interests or just having time to ourselves. $|\rangle - \text{a.yrg}.$

On the academic front, the girls get through 12 to 20 pieces of work a week, two to four each morning. Subjects currently being worked on include English, History, Geography, Religious Studies, and Human Biology with topics in Childcare, Environment and Conservation, Community Studies, other Sciences and some Maths. The programme may seem rather structured but there is substantial flexibility within it.

Some recent examples of work will perhaps be useful:

The Gulf Crisis
The girls produces their own file on the Gulf. A cross-subjects approach was adopted with work on the geography of the area, the history and religion of Islam, and the environmental effects of the war. The current plight of he Kurds is being looked at.

Human Biology
This is the most natural science for young people for it is about themselves. The girls chose this and they have increased in enthusiasm for the subject since they began it a year ago. Interest and progress in this subject will probably mean they will be up to GCSE standard by the time they are 14. It is a subject that overlaps with animal and plant biology that may lead into other areas later.
                    $GCSE - 14 \text{ y/s}!$
Maths
We have long held the view that the emphasis, or near obsession with mathematics and numeracy within the education system is not only unnecessary but largely counter-productive. Such an abstract and theoretical subject could better be left until 10 or 12 before being treated to the intense attention currently lavished on it at all ages. Needless to say our daughters do less formal maths than a school would, but in fact approach the subject with a healthy interest. Some recent 'back door' approaches have included looking at the history of coins, geography work on scales, looking at statistics and charts relating to the current census as well as designing and playing heir own games involving financial transactions and numbers.

A variety of other links and approaches are planned including those between music, architecture, art perspective and geometry. Who says maths is boring?

Our daughters afternoon programme includes art, music, pottery and other crafts, and cooking. Tina's skills in the artistic field dominate here. Frequent 'hands on' experience and practice, always with supervision for safety, has led to enormous jumps in skill levels and confidence. Afternoons are about serious enjoyment and fun. Afternoons may also be about some physical activity: games on the common or walks on the hills. Again the structure and programme are flexible; again the girls have a say in what is selected and done.

Supporting this am/pm week are a variety of activities and interests involving the family and others. The Easter vacation, for example, has seen the girls involved in a three day stay with grandparents, walks and expeditions on the hills, frequent playing sessions with friends, a day visit to an activities camp, obtaining a Red Cross First Aid certificate and various other outings.

The list of summer activities is even longer and wider (deliberately so): trips to various museums, a farm, castles, a fire station, visits to and from relations and a mountain expedition - to mention but a few - mostly chosen by the girls.

Questions people ask

Are we anti-school or the 'system'?
Yes and No is the answer. We have certainly not been impressed by the quality of some teaching. Neither have we been impressed with the increasing volume of administrative and political interference present in school. And the level of bureaucratic self-interest within 'the system' is appalling, given the task to which all are supposed to be devoted.

Despite these comments, we still consider there to be things of worth within formal education. A good teacher is a delight to watch and a considerable asset to any institution and society as a whole. My own years in education have shown me again and again that there are many dedicated and talented people working in schools and colleges. Many of our educational facilities and personnel deserve our appreciation and encouragement - particularly those involved in the many areas of special needs.

Being a teacher, do my wife and I follow the National Curriculum?
No - although we are abreast of developments and consider that despite some things of worth in the National Curriculum, it is very limiting and prescriptive. In some respects, the wrong subjects are being taught at the wrong age and in the wrong way. A simplified comment, perhaps, but we believe still valid.

Whatever current education is, or is becoming, it is, in our view, not going in the right direction.

Are we over-protective as parents?
This is a common question, and one often linked to the 'are we not depriving our children of social contact and friends of their own age' argument. No, is the answer. If we take parenting seriously then we must take society seriously. Children do not exist in a vacuum and it is entirely in appropriate to wrap them in cotton wool. A well thought out home-based education (and quite probably *any* home-based education) provides many opportunities for social contact.

When we look at the enormous range of social contacts (formal and informal) our daughters have, that question falls flat. And when we see the diversity of community activities they have been involved in, it is hardly surprising that they are better socially adjusted and responsive than most school pupils are.

Do we have specific aims for our daughters' education?
Yes, is the answer - and not just the more tangible (but distant) one of five, ten or whatever GCSEs. Academic success in a number of subjects is already on the horizon, and we have no immediate concern in this area. More important is the emotional, spiritual development of our children: that they grow up to be well-balanced, caring and thoughtful young and adult people is paramount in our thinking. Also important is that they be given the chance of a genuinely broad education - not artificially limited by the restrictions of syllabus requirements and politics.

In our view, learning takes place all the time - not because 'teacher' or an institution says so. Add to that a home environment that fosters opportunities and encourages enquiring, and you have a far more effective and more natural learning situation than schools can provide. There has to be more to 'learning' than the production-line mentality currently dominating educational theory and practice.

Are we, as parents, confident that we are doing the right thing for our daughters?
Yes, is the answer, and for a variety of reasons:

- We have seen the changes in our daughters - and they are all for the good. Gone are the distortions and stresses imposed (intentionally or

20

otherwise) by schooling. Returned to us is the energy, enthusiasm and spontaneity of young people liberated from the tyranny of petty regimes.

- We can structure an informal programme to individual interests and need. Thus idealistic aims such as those found in official documents, such as the 1944 Education Act, and the expressed wish to provide education according to age, aptitude and ability, have a greater ring of truth in the home situation that they do in many schools. We can make a reality of adapting and improving idea and resources to suit the age, aptitude and ability of our children.

- The opportunities for their education are now so much more diverse. Access to equipment and resources are not restricted nor progress hindered by the restrictions of lesson time, syllabus, disruptive pupils or teacher's interests. There has probably never been a better time to home-educate. The range and quality of resources available to parents is amazing. The problem becomes one of knowing what to select or to budget for - although much can be acquired through libraries, resource centres and on free loan from companies.

Summary

The more we work with and observe our daughters, the more aware we are that much of the educating is done by them, not us.

Like all young people they have an impressive capacity to acquire, organise or make 'their sense' of the world about them. We aim to provide an environment where those natural abilities thrive and where understanding and skills are nurtured - not force fed.

We do not suggest that our approach is the right way to educate children, but it is our way. We do not envisage that it will not change, we hope it does. We hope we are always looking for better and/or different ways of approaching subjects, improving resources and questioning our aims. It is, after all, that healthy variety of approach that is so characteristic of home-based education and contrast so sharply with the 'monoculture' of the state and private sectors.

Update

One of the advantages of a home-based education should be the variety of opportunities on offer. Life in general should also be viewed as creating, or seizing upon opportunities on offer. So it is within recent weeks we have been offered the opportunity to take charge of a small school - or, to be more accurate, a group of children whose parents have all opted to educate their sons or daughters 'other than by attendance at school'. Thus our home-based and 'otherwise' experience is now being utilised in a wider context.

Does this mean that we have now dropped the idea of home-based education? Have we compromised our stand against much of formal education?

A resounding NO is the answer. After long and careful consideration, and discussion with our daughters, we viewed the change as a valuable educational opportunity - both for our family and for others. We will continue with the informal programme and approach developed over the past two years. We will also now introduce other youngsters to that experience and the resources that have been built up.

We are aware of the dangers of being gradually sucked into the formal school scenario. Therefore, we will carefully guard what is special and unique about the family and small group situation.

We will not play the National Curriculum or Common Entrance game, but will continue to take what is good or useful from any source as well as following our own course. We will not become burdened with a mountain of administrative chores, but will continue to be highly organised and methodical to be better able to encourage and motivate.

Most of all, we will not succumb to the temptation of trying to be good at everything. It is not possible or even desirable. What we will do, though, is play to strengths and to our vision - and keep a friendly light burning in the window for other families of similar persuasion.

Acknowledgement

A version of this article first appeared in Education Otherwise, Number 80, June 1991

Putting together
a home-based education package

by Pip Rupik

As a result of my work with the Children's Home-based Education Association over the last three years, I have come to believe more and more that a great many of the problems that beset individual families, and our education system in general, stem from the mistaken belief that the education of a child is the responsibility of the school and/or the Local Education Authority and/or the State. So much legislation in recent years seems to have been based on this misunderstanding of the 1944 Education Act, which is itself the basis of all other educational legislation since that date.

Section 36 of the 1944 Act gives PARENTS the prime responsibility to provide their children with an *"efficient full-time education suitable to his age, ability and aptitude, and to any special educational needs he may have."* Section 765 places an obligation on the Minister and the L.E.A. to have regard to the wishes of the parent. However, almost all legislation since that date, although going some way to acknowledging the participation of the parent, is drawn up with the assumption that professionals know best and that really it is they that should direct the way.

Voting with their feet

Children are voting with their feet when they truant. Yet in my experience, the almost universal reaction from L.E.A's is that of FORCING non-attenders back to school by various tactics including threats of care orders and sending parents to prison.

However, the families that come to me with problems of attendance are able to find a suitable solution once they are aware of their rights and all the options open to them in their own particular situation. It takes little imagination to project that into the realisation that any families who lose court cases would not do so if they were simple aware of their rights and options, and would be able to find a solution that suited them and that provided their children with a full-time, efficient education.

My experience leads me to propose that the key to the problem is not FORCING children into whatever situation they feel is straightjacketing them, but in acknowledging that each family is quite capable of providing the child with an efficient, full-time education, once all options have been laid before them.

Time and again, heads of colleges and adult and open learning centres defend their reluctance to take under-16's by saying that it would open the floodgates and the state school system would be in tatters. Already we see around us a system where so many are tired of swimming against the tide that they give up, be they teachers, children or parents. Those responsible for administering the system are spending the very public money in mopping up the symptoms that could, and should, be spent creatively.

So many people involved in education, and not least the consumers who are voting with their feet, would create a better situation, both in general and for each individual family, if they were not straightjacketed into reinforcing a lie. The 1994 Act gives PARENTS the prime responsibility to direct the course of their children's education, and LEA's the responsibility to provide the resources in order that the PARENT can fulfil that duty.

We know that much enthusiasm and creativity abounds in the area of education, but so much of it is frustrated by inflexible bureaucracy and red tape. I find that parents want to be involved in the process of allowing that creativity and enthusiasm to bear fruit. My experience is that parents would love a FLEXIBLE system where their children could perhaps spend part of their 'school' career at home, full-time, for a period of their life; another period in full-time school or college or another centre; another in combination with the two; the CHOICE being there, when and if their situation dictated the need.

The barrier of conditioning

The desire for a home-based approach is there on all sides, and so is the basic legislation that would allow every family to put together their own package if they chose to. The obstacles are many and varied. Perhaps the greatest and most far-reaching is conditioning. Most people in the U.K. are brought up to believe that school equals education, therefore education equals school; that 'home-based education' means that the child is isolated and restricted when in fact the whole world is now their classroom; that professionals are the most competent.

I believe that the way to show that these conditioned beliefs are not true in reality is also home-based. Parents and children are already voting with their feet and so creating a demand. People out there are already saying 'I would like to meet that demand if you give me a chance.' Almost all parents who come to me are amazed that the conditioning that they have received is based on untruths. They are amazed and elated (and relieved) that it isn't a simple case of state full-time versus private full-time.

Parents are thrilled to learn that it is possible to put together a 'home-based package' perhaps with the help of individual professionals or some kind of centre, school, group or college, or totally from their own skills. They are thrilled to hear that I am an ordinary working-class mum who left school at fifteen with no qualifications and took my children to GCSE level at home, and that hundreds of families have been just as successful at putting together their own home-based package.

Making rights and options known

My role within the C.H.E.A. and as a writer is not to place value judgements on any particular kind of education system. It is simply to give parents as much information as I have on the options that exist in their own particular case, to try to boost their confidence in their own abilities if that is lacking, and then to credit them with enough intelligence to make their own decisions and with enough ability and commitment to bring it to reality.

The C.H.E.A. continues to campaign for a legal obligation to be placed on L.E.A.'s to inform parents of their rights and options before legal action is taken regarding any child. This is a basic human right, you might think, but it is one the Government is reluctant to implement.

A great shift overnight in demands for a more flexible system supplied by the state, would cause some problems. Yet the Government's aiding and abetting of the present increase in parents demands for more say and more active participation can achieve a gradual turnaround. As more parents go to schools and colleges and request a more flexible package and are turned down, only to go away and successfully put together such a package themselves, the message will get through. Some bright spark will see political profit in campaigning for or providing what the public are demanding.

The Children's Home-based Education Association, of which I am the General Secretary, is an organisation for all parents who wish to be involved in their children's education, whether the children are educated at school, at home, or in some combination of the two. Much of our time is spent campaigning for, and protecting the rights and options of parents and children in education, as well as helping parents to discover all the options available to them.

Providing vital information

In response to the demand for information from parents, I am also compiling a Flexible Learning Directory for Children up to Sixteen to be published by Apronstrings Education. This is aimed at providing parents with details of all the options open to them in their own area so that they can put together their personalised package. It is made up of details of schools and centres offering education after school hours, during school hours, full-time, part-time, flexischooling, open learning, distance learning, groups, workshops, private tutors etc. The choice is then for the parents and the children to make. I am also compiling a publication for Apronstrings pointing out general options and some ideas regarding what to look for when deciding.

The demand for direct participation by the home is there and growing. The resources are available. If we help families to go on voting with their feet, I really believe we can make it come together.

Pip Rupik is a writer on educational matters and may be contacted at
14 Basil Avenue, Armthorpe, Doncaster, South Yorkshire DN3 2AR

Case studies of children learning at home.

by Julie Webb

Stimulated by curiosity as to the 'results' of home-based education (I was considering home educating my son), I set out in 1982, as an Open University Ph.D. student, to interview home educating families with teenagers who could be followed over the next few years into their chosen work or further education. The original twenty participating families finally became twenty seven, to include some single parents and commune dwellers. I also interviewed various LEA officers, a headmistress and a teacher trainer, herself home educated in the 1930's.

My interest in what became of home educated children in adult life soon expanded into one encompassing the whole process of home educating: the reasons for undertaking it, what the curriculum consisted of and how it was pursued in terms of both methods and resources, what relationships families had with the rest of the community and with their LEA and what, if any, the implications of all this might be for orthodox education.

I shall discuss here some of the most interesting point to emerge. (Those who would like a more detailed discussion will find one in the book, *Children learning at home,* Falmer Press, 1990.

The reasons people gave for home educating were in most cases related to unhappiness in school, where children had suffered from an inappropriate curriculum, or bullying by fellow pupils or teachers, or where they had fallen out with the authorities over some aspect of the school's regime (for example a boy of Scots parentage who had always worn a kilt with other elements of school uniform, and who was suddenly prevented from doing this by his new head). Idealistic home educators with objections to the principles of the education system were less well represented among the families I talked to than is generally the case nowadays in Education Otherwise, where they tend to be parents of younger children. What appeared to be significant though, is the extent to which objections in principle began to develop among my interviewees after they had received an inflexible and unsympathetic response to their children's problems in school. Interesting too, was the reinforcement which these families provided of other researchers' findings that teachers form a large group of those teaching their children at home. I concluded that, (as

27

one of the teacher mothers I interviewed confirmed in her own case) knowledge of the school processes from the inside led many to want something different for their own children and to be prepared to provide it if, having given school a chance, a change was necessary.

Increasing confidence

Many of the families made the decision to home educate without much confidence in their ability to organise an area of life formerly organised for them, and without the support that is nowadays available from organisations such as Education Otherwise and CHEA (Children's Home-based Education Association). In most cases, however, their confidence in what they were doing grew as they got more used to being actively in charge of it. This was reflected in some of the changes which took place in their choice of learning activities and ways to carry them out.

Families often began by imitating the method and content of a school curriculum, and to give themselves a reassuring structure on which to base their work. These school-like features usually disappeared as confidence grew and children were encouraged to concentrate on their own special interests, whether at home or elsewhere in the community. A more naturally structured and more flexible use of time also began to establish itself, related to the fixed points of the children's outside activities and the commitments of family life.

Family intentions

The families' aims in home educating were another important influence on the 'what' and 'how' of their practice. All saw the achievement of basic literacy and numeracy as important, and most continued to insist on the daily rehearsal of these even when the children had a more or less free choice as to which other activities they pursued. Many aimed for GCE's as they were then, with a view to further or higher education: most of the teenagers had considered and realistic views about what future work they would enjoy and be suited to. The requirements of GCE courses were often tackled through a take-what-you-need-and leave-the-rest approach to correspondence courses or FE colleges, autonomy and self-discipline being well developed in most families by the time exams loomed.

Where families were not pursuing formal qualifications, their aim was often to allow children to explore any interest they might have, whatever their apparent ability, taking advantage of freedom from timetables and the prescribed curriculum which may restrict choice in school.

Resourcefulness

Choosing what to learn and how to learn it want hand in hand with looking for appropriate resources, and there was very little evidence that lack of the kinds of resources available in school had a constraining effect on the home curriculum. Science, for example, is often cited as the academic area in which school facilities are essentials, but in fact the interviewees found that physics and biology could be followed up to GCE O level using ordinary household equipment and recommended textbooks.

For chemistry and A level sciences, part-time attendance at school or FE college, or the use of institutional lab facilities after hours, solved the problem. Community dance and drama groups, orchestras, museums, libraries, art and craft and sports centres, subject-based local societies and adult education classes, as well as all the informal possibilities of the working world, proved a huge number of opportunities for following existing academic and non-academic interests and for stimulating new ones. Open-mindedness and determination seem to be the home educating family's most important resources.

The extensive use which nearly all of those interviewed made of community resources suggests that the picture of social isolation presented to the public mind by the home educated child may not be accurate, particularly now that a large and active network of home educators exists. The teenagers I talked to were exceptionally articulate, self-confident and sociable, with an ability to get on with people of all ages, and had no lack of friends (except in the case of one girl, who was the eldest of several children living in a commune.)

It appeared to me that self-esteem and understanding of a wide range of people's feelings and attitudes might be more important factors in sociability than lengthy exposure to a large group of one's peers.

Variable LEA policy

I also investigated home educators' relationships with their LEA's. LEA policy on treatment of families seemed to vary within their area and from officer to officer, a reflection of the lack of experience then characteristic of their dealings with home educators and perhaps of the scope for varied interpretation of the relevant laws. The impression, given by those heavily publicised families whose relationships with their LEA is hostile, is that all LEA's are "out to get" home educators, was not justified by the evidence of those families who had established at least neutral, sometimes positively helpful, relationships with their authorities.

Perhaps LEAs are themselves partly responsible for the suspicion with which they are treated: if they were willing to suggest home-based education as an option which they would support in appropriate circumstances, more open relationships might develop which could benefit both parties. (1)

Making the most of opportunities

To return to the question with which I began this research: what do home educated children make of their adult lives? Only half of those interviewed replied to follow-up letters and, of these, none were older than twenty four, so my comments need to be read with these observations in mind.

All those who applied for further or higher education courses were admitted to them, sometimes on the strength of personality and a simple maths and English test alone, where they lacked the relevant formal qualifications. Courses taken ranged from catering and agriculture City and Guilds, to university degrees in forestry, mathematics, drama and geography.

Those who wanted to work found it, again in widely varying fields: working at a boarding kennel, and broadcasting in the USA were two examples. Most of those who kept in touch appeared to have a conventional attitude to work: only one had rejected the work ethic, and in her case voluntary work in the community, and self-expression through writing and music, took the place of employment.

It seemed to me from all this evidence that home education does not have to be, as some have suggested, a barrier to leading a full life in the ordinary world; and that it may equip people to make the most of their opportunities very well, in fact. Further research in ten years should provide more interesting and extensive information on this.

For the education system, the most important message to emerge from this study is that of the need for greater flexibility, whether to enable unhappy children to carry on more happily in State schools, to enable their parents to negotiate flexischooling or to set up their own small schools, or to educate at home with greater support. This results in precisely the sort of person, able to respond flexibly, which we require for working, living and being fulfilled in the world today. The teenagers were exceptionally articulate, self-confident and sociable.

* * * * *

(1) Some recent evidence from families educating their children at home suggests that a number of LEAs now have a more positive and cooperative approach

Making home-based education a normal and available option for all

by Bruce Cox

Imagine a society controlled from the centre through a vast bureaucracy. Its leaders see themselves as benevolent, but the masses for whom they make choices seem strangely sullen, responsive to voices of dissent and symbols of resistance.

The leaders decide to clarify the rules. Acting in the same spirit as those who use volume as an aid to understanding for the deaf and foreigners, they stake out the path the ideal citizen must take through life. Supervision is tightened. Dissenters are maginalised, harassed, labelled as crazy or dangerous or failures.

Now, is this a sketch of Eastern Europe before the thaw ... or of British Education?

Curious contradictions

How ironic that a government that prides itself on freedom of choice, now introduces policies which ordain both the ends of education, the national curriculum, and the means by which they are to be achieved, schooling, whilst simultaneously inveighing against the 'nanny' state. The Economy is to grow by leaving people alone, abolishing central controls and letting the market decide. The education system, whose primary aim for the state is the servicing of the Economy, is increasingly to be controlled from the centre. We may have any breakfast cereal we choose and have any from of education we fancy so long as it is a school.

Of course, there are small holes in the monolith. *Education Otherwise* is one of them. It is possible for parents to educate their children outside of school. My own three children have spent most of their 'school age' lives outside of schools - a fact that, in spite of all the trials and problems, I rejoice in.

But our society is not structured to make home-based education an easy option. Schools deprive EO children of most of their fellows, from nine to four, most days. There is no incentive for the provision of any social or educational

32

facilities during these hours. Reactions vary from supportive, *"You're so lucky, I wish I had known about it,"* to alarmed, *"Those poor children, they've got to face the real world some time,"* to alarming, *"I do admire you. You are so brave. I couldn't do it."*

Often the prelude to home-based education is misery at school so that the need to recover from unhappiness and perceived failure compounds other problems. No EO parent, even those who are financially well-off - and most are not - can be unaware that they are swimming against the tide and that it is hard work.

The value of support

This is what makes the national support network, *Education Otherwise*, so important. Parents are pulled or driven towards EO by powerful feelings, fuelled by strong ideals or desperate problems, but the impetus can be difficult to maintain. So many people who have discovered EO have reported their relief, their relaxation, their sheer gratitude at finding that it exists and that it contains for everyone at least some kindred spirits. For the children, too, the sense of tribal identity in belonging to EO is deeply satisfying. Our children have built lasting friendships, all over the country as well as locally.

Since its beginnings in 1977, the organisation has developed into a model for a national self-help group. It achieves a great deal on small income simply because of the active participation of so many members.

Vulnerability and doubts

I remember, some years ago, hearing by chance that EO friends who lived nearby, with several children similar in age to our own, were planning to send them to school. My feelings were then ones of betrayal and despair, tinged with exhaustion. Even then, I was aware that my reaction was a bit extreme. It revealed to me how vulnerable and ambivalent I felt, at that time, about the children's education. Were they learning enough? Could home-based education be sustained without a local network of like-minded families? Later, two of my own children went to a Steiner school on a part-time basis and I know that some of my own EO friends had the same reaction to me.

I would not react in the same way today. The children are older. If they seem all right in the present, I feel no reason to worry how they will 'turn out'. Two of the children started, at their own choice, full time schooling in their mid-teens. For them, it seemed an appropriate step. They coped with little difficulty, in spite of having had very little formal instruction before going - confirming my belief that most of the learning ascribed to the actions of teachers is mainly a by-product of growing up in our society, a realisation which the universality of schooling prevents most of us from reaching.

Practitioners of EO soon become aware of its benefits and develop the skills of responding with practiced ease to the questions they are constantly asked. These responses are genuine but there are, of course, problems. However, most of these are not intrinsic to EO; they arise from society which does not expect or cater for home education.

The road to changing this is a long one. *Education Otherwise* itself can do only a limited amount. It is not set up to be a campaigning body. Understandably, most of its energy must be directed to finding ways of helping its members to cope within the existing system. EO parents have enough to do without campaigning for political changes which may never materialise. We are like mice living in a land of dinosaurs, waiting for evolution to take its course.

However, for those with the will and energy to pursue them, there are changes in the public sphere which, if made, could enable a more humane and varied system to develop.

Possible changes

I will mention three measures, all of them possible, none of them involving an increase in public spending.

The first would entail minor changes, legalising part-time registration of pupils at schools wishing to offer this facility. Schools would be allowed pro-rata capitation for such pupils. At present, part-time schooling is rarely found. It is not a right and where it does exist does so on a grace and favour basis. This change would only involve schools which choose to take part but would begin to dissolve the schools' temporal and coercive boundaries. The second change would involve the establishment of a well-resourced distance learning centre, paid for in whole or part by the state. Children could be registered with this centre as an alternative to conventional schooling. This change would undermine the pernicious confusion of 'education' with 'attendance'. It would enable thousands of teenagers who would never dream of dropping out of school without such support to escape from unhappiness and failure of underachievement within schools.

The third change would enable small groups of parents to set up small schools, not necessarily permanent, paid for by the state at the same per capita rate as state schools, with the minimum of vetting.

If the structure of the system were loosened to allow more choice, I would hope to see a greater variety of all kinds of schools, a vast increase in part-time schooling mixed with out-of-school education, and a growing custom of parents taking children out of school for substantial periods simply to get to know them better, to enjoy their company and to do things together that the demands of schooling squeeze out.

Perhaps, eventually, significant educational choice will be seen as central to our society and our democracy. Although schools seem to be like shells from which life and inspiration have drained away, they still appear powerful, monolithic, permanent; but then, so did the state bureaucracies of the Eastern Bloc. Both are bankrupt structures, sustained by the denial of choices and the stifling of alternatives.

Perhaps the comparison with the Eastern Bloc is far-fetched. It sprung to mind because many EO families have the experience of being defined as dissidents. They may be strengthened and invigorated by this but they also pay a price. If you have strong beliefs which society marginalises, you become identified with those beliefs on terms defined by the powerful. Vaclav Havel becomes more politician than playwright, Sakharov becomes more dissident than physicist. How often do EO parents, on a less heroic scale, have to organise their lives to revolve around home education so that, to others, this becomes their distinguishing social characteristic, a shorthand sign by which they may be identified?

I hope that the second phase in the growth of education otherwise will begin when the children of today's EO parents are old enough for their parents and allies to have time to work towards creating conditions for the next generation to have wider choice of alternatives and a stronger structure of support. The struggle for such conditions will have to have a political dimension

Home-based education is business as usual: what we learn from children's experiences in their first five years.

by Janet Meighan

The importance of the first five years of life is now universally recognised. The extent of growth and development during these years is perhaps unequalled in any other period in life. In the process of exploring and 'finding out' about their world, young children acquire the skills and understanding on which later learning will be based. Their learning is fuelled by their curiosity, enjoyment and satisfaction, which evolve from a basis of security and confidence. And those holding the key to effective learning in these years are the PARENTS and families.

Successive governments have upheld the importance of parents' role in ruling that statutory entry to schooling shall be five years, and in failing to provide nursery education for all who seek it. As a teacher of young children for many years, I have marvelled at the understanding these young people display on entering school, the range of skills they exhibit, and the diversity of their individuality. How do families pull off these remarkable achievements?

Learning with our children

Before my first son was born, in common with many young parents to be, I had a very limited view of how I would be involved in his early learning. Nor did I have clear expectations about everything he might learn. This was in spite of taking my impending parenthood seriously by reading on the subject and discussing ideas with others. In the event, I learnt from him; observing his actions and responding to his needs. Mistakes were inevitably made and valuable opportunities for learning lost, but reflecting on my own experiences, and those of other parents of young children, highlighted some of the important contributions we make to our young children's learning at home.

- We are able to ensure a secure base for their confidence building.

- There are opportunities to share their experiences, their enjoyment and fun.

- We acknowledge and encourage their achievements, appreciating their efforts in solving problems and decision making, and supporting their developing autonomy.

- We recognise the importance, at times, of our adult model, yet try to respond positively to their curiosity as they explore their world.

- We learn not to interfere too much in their learning, appreciating that they need their own 'space'. However, we seek to be available to offer help and advice when this is asked for.

- We try to extend their experience of the world through the opportunities we make available to them.

- We recognise and take into account their individuality - their interests, challenges and problems, pace of learning, personality...

A longer list could be made! But even accounting for the differences that occur between parents and families due to life-style, health, quality of housing, income...we all share the experience of learning with and from our children during the first five years. Given that our children achieve such milestones as learning to walk, talk, dress, feed...and may be well on the road to becoming future scientists, musicians, artists mathematicians...we parents are a hard act to follow!

Lessons for all

Because home-based education in these early years is seen as the norm it receives scant attention, unless difficulties arise for particular families. Many nursery and infant schools make great efforts to build on the learning achieved at home, working closely with parents to ensure a continuing personalised approach to education.

But as they grow older, what happens to those motivated young people with their insatiable curiosity, who have shown growing independence and autonomy in directing their own learning, and who in the words of John Holt act *"... like scientists all the time, which is to say, looking, noticing, wondering, theorizing, testing their theories and changing them as often as they have to."*? What does our education system do to them? What lessons are there so be learnt from their early education at home?

Yes, home-based education is business as usual, not closed, but open all hours and still flourishing!

Educated for life by life itself

by Collette Bradley

I always knew that I would not subject my son to the rigours of school life at a very young age and so I educated him at home until he was just seven.

Home education is total commitment. In our case it meant a loss of potential earning power and the struggle to live on just one, not very reliable income. In retrospect, I would do it all again as those seven years, although at times exhausting and difficult, were never boring.

To witness and nurture the natural curiosity of one's child is to experience the greatest joy. To be able to follow a child's interests without the straightjacket of school timetables is wonderful and I had a deep conviction that my son was missing nothing by being at home in a safe, loving and secure environment

My approach to the three 'Rs' was a fairly organised one. We did 'lessons' three times a week. These would take place at a double school desk with both of us sitting on tiny wooden chairs side by side. I used various teaching aids and schemes and decided to introduce a reading scheme. Seth had always loved books because I did but I hesitated about a scheme and introduced it with great trepidation. Seth loved the books and was excited to move up the levels in his own time. In fact, the scheme worked wonderfully for us - we used Ginn Readers - and when he reached level 8 he was reading fluently and it seemed time to stop bothering with the graded books. On some mornings we would be busily involved for as long as three hours, including breaks for snacks, listening to education programmes on Radio 5, using the Dacta materials (Technic Lego Technology), doing science experiments, cooking ... the list is long and varied.

The advantages of home-based learning over school learning are many. One has a far greater freedom of choice and movement out of school. An interesting topic can be followed for as long as enthusiasm lasts. The child has ample time for quiet activity and the pressures to conform are absent. The quality of concentration in a quiet environment must be better than in a class of 30 other children therefore learning at home is done more speedily than in school.

We lived in a suburban area where we were the only home-educating family for miles. I worked hard to establish contacts with as many families as I could and for four years was the Co-ordinator of *Education Otherwise* in West Sussex. Unfortunately there was very little response in West Sussex, so we teamed up with the folks in East Sussex and travelled many miles and many hours to get to meetings. Sometimes it involved an overnight stay. Seth made good friends through our group meetings and we once travelled as far as Newcastle to be with other E.O. families. Our activities included canoeing, camping, candle making, paper making, drama, music, inumerable long walks and picnics.

Our monthly trips to London took us to the Science, Geographical and Natural History Museums and once even to a Piere Cardin exhibition at the Victoria and Albert where we giggled over the ludicrous creations. Seth imbibed my love of the big city and our visits were always lots of fun and very interesting. We indulged in people-watching, boating on the Thames and negotiating the London bus routes and the Underground.

What a glory to be educated for life by life itself!

The time came for my son to move on , out of the home and away from the companionship of his mother. He chose a school which was 170 miles away from where we lived. We loved the school and decided to move house. The school operates in a way of which we approve, being child-centred, small, extremely friendly and positively needing parental involvement. Seth enjoys it greatly and settled in quickly and easily. The bright light in his eyes continues to shine and despite my feelings of loss, I feel we have done the best thing. But we remain open.

With one learner happy at school, one happy to be now learning at home, and a third coming out of school to become a home-based learner, the Downing family demonstrates how flexischooling works for them.

Making it work both in and out of school

by Wendy Downing

As a family, we are partly within the regular education system and partly with *Education Otherwise*. I have three children, Leigh aged 16, Jody 13, and Emmalyne 12. We only discovered that *Education Otherwise* existed fairly recently.

Until last year, the children were in small private schools, Leigh and Emmalyne were fine, but Jody was not. They are all individuals and, as such, they differ. Jody was withdrawn from the private system and placed in the local Senior School. At first she was miserable but is now very happy with it. She has grown into a young lady with interests in pop music, clothes and the opposite sex. She has always gravitated towards children we'd rather she didn't and the plethora of these in the State System is to her liking.

Leigh hates school and is resentful of the fact that we discovered *Education Otherwise* too late for him to opt out of the system. He sat his GCSE's at school but now plans to do 'A' levels at home. Leigh is not a 'tough' character and he has been bullied throughout his secondary school life. The school has a new headteacher who is splendid, caring, keen and able, however, he cannot beat the system that sends him so many pupils and expects miracle from him.

When Emmalyne was forced to leave the small private school for financial reasons, I was perturbed. She is a very private person who is bright and able. At her first school, her high I.Q. was prized and respected and she was popular with staff and pupils alike. She achieved well and was a very happy little girl. A State secondary school nearly destroyed her.

She was verbally and physically persecuted for being a 'swat' and a 'snob'. My lovely daughter began having nightmares, was foul-tempered and obviously depressed. When I heard about *Education Otherwise* and its legality, a light broke through the storm clouds in my heart.

Emmalyne wants to be a vet or a lawyer and so must study formal subjects for GCSE. We do about 18 hours of solidly academic work each week and she spends the rest of her time walking, visiting places of interest, riding her pony, caring for a variety of animals, gardening, doing pottery, reading etc. She has a few close friends whom she sees regularly. My daughter is back with me, diligent and delightful as she was before. Her smile light up frequently, sparking my own feelings of happiness for her.

Replies to criticism

Unsolicited criticism is rife, usually of the *"What about socialisation?"* or *"How do you teach Maths and/or Science?"* variety. We live in a world of many types of human being and varying ages. My daughter has some good friends. She also has contact with life in general, on a daily basis. She is of help to various local farmers, and knows people of all ages and social classes. She has close friends older than her parents and also some younger than herself.

Emmalyne's sister Jody enjoys the rough and tumble of school life claiming it is her scene. She is happy there and that is her choice. Emmalyne is happy away from it and I support her choice equally.

When people question my ability to teach her, I usually say that I managed well enough when she was younger. Sometimes I ask them if they doubt my intelligence - a retort designed to confound! I have either obtained suitable literature and swotted it up as we went along, or in one case I made arrangements for a tutor to take her on a regular basis for individual French lessons. And, if you cannot envisage coping with the teaching yourself, there are correspondence courses available, that are not too expensive.

The cost of home-based education in general is another query. We are not rich, so we have to keep the expenses as low as possible. Books can be obtained from the local library or bought second-hand. I have had to turn down a lucrative employment offer as I could not find the time but I consider my daughter's happiness more important to me than the pursuit of wealth. I brought her into the world and I feel that I should make her world as good as it can be for her until she has the where-with-all to care for herself.

I believe that children have human rights and that these include the right to choose how they receive their education. I am allowing my children to make that choice by supporting their different individual decisions. I only regret that I did not know that it was possible to do so in time for my son to have benefited. I hope that my children will feel that they have made good decisions and that other parents will do the same for their children.

* * * * *

P.S. Emmalyne subsequently gained six GCSE's with impressive grades.

Adult chauvinism and children's rights

by Patrick Pringle

I have brought up and not 'educated' all my four children with varying results. None of them ever stepped inside a school or had a day's tutition at home, and no attempt was ever made to persuade them to learn anything, although all were exposed to lots of books, from comics to Encyclopaedia Britannica.

My fourth child, Patrick, may interest you most. At the age of thirteen, he was still innumerate and fairly ignorant of almost everything except birds, which he loved to watch and read about. Yet before he was fourteen he had passed GCSE in four subjects and only the November examination clashes stopped him from taking six.

I do not think he is specially gifted, but he has a strong career motivation. His early interest in birds spread to wildlife in general and then to ecology; and after meeting David Bellamy he too wanted to become an environmental scientist to help save the world.

Being too myopic to tell a pigeon from Concorde, and totally ignorant of science, I could not even answer questions and contributed only by buying books and equipment like a chemistry set and a microscope. I think he succeeded in GCSE because he was sufficiently interested to spend nine months of his life studying all day and half the night. I can only claim that I did not try to stop him, just as I had not tried to stop him before from idling his life away.

He is taking life more easily now. In a few weeks he will sit his other two GCSE exams (and three of the other four to try for higher grades). He plans to take 3 or 4 'A' level exams in two years time when he is sixteen. Then he hopes to go to university or polytechnic if we can find one willing to admit him at that age.

He cannot, however, continue to be an autodidact. He could have done if he had studied, for example, modern languages (which would probably have been easier, as his mother is German and he was born and bred in Spain and then lived in France); but he chose science, and although his home laboratory, although adequate for GCSE, cannot be upgraded to 'A' levels because I cannot afford an oscilloscope and even quite harmless chemicals have become publicly unavailable. Happily, although rejected as too young by further education colleges, he has been accepted for a two year 'A' level course by a Sixth Form Centre for over-16's although he is only fourteen, and they are such marvellous dedicated people that he is keenly looking forward to classwork experience.

As you will doubtless inferred, I am a bit of an anarchist and a children's rights extremist, a disciple of Toltsoi and Illich and A.S.Neill. I believe adult chauvinism should be denounced and truancy decriminalised. But I am also 72, and doubtless have a touch of Altzheimer's, or I would be writing another book (I've published 70) about all this myself. Instead I hope these brief notes may add a mite to your further studies in what I hope will prove to be the educational pathway of the future.

World-wide Education Service Home School: recent developments in the U.K.

by Dorrie Wheldall

The work of the WES Home School lies in offering support to English-speaking parents who are educating their own children. The majority of these parents are living overseas and decide to educate their children because there are no suitable school in the vicinity. For most, the possibility of sending them to boarding school does not offer a real alternative as they prefer to stay together as a family unit.

Although many of our families are overseas we have long been aware of the growing interest in the U.K. concerning home education. We have been considering how we can use our many years of experience with parents living overseas in order to help families in this country whose needs are similar in many respects. They may differ, however, in their reasons for home education, choosing to educate their children for a variety of philosophical, religious, social or moral reasons; geographical location playing a minor role.

Services to U.K. families

In assessing the needs of U.K. families, we have taken into account the fact that, as well as generally being more confident in their abilities, they also have access to a network of support services and contact with other families. Therefore, they will not necessarily require our tutorial service which is so important for overseas families, many of whom may be fairly isolated. We are also conscious of economic constraints and the fact that U.K. families will be financing themselves.

WES Home School U.K. offers a wide choice of Primary curriculum courses whereby parents can opt to follow the whole curriculum, individual subjects or a group of subjects. Books and materials to support the curriculum may be obtained independently or through WES, as desired. At the present time, independent courses are available for children aged 7-11 years. Courses for younger children are now being developed and will be available later next year.

The teaching notes assume no previous teaching experience on the part of the parent as full guidance in the various subject areas explain how and what to teach. More general details about the organisation and management of the Home School are also included e.g. planning lessons, timetabling. presentation of work, motivation, assessment and recording. These ensure that parents are able to follow the courses quite independently whilst teaching their children to a high standard. However, should they require it, there is an additional advisory and tutorial service available.

The WES curriculum

The WES courses take into account the National Curriculum, although we appreciate that home schooling families are not required to follow this. We have chosen to include it as many of our overseas families will eventually return to the U.K. and will then often place their children into mainstream schools. U.K. families, at some stage, may also wish to send their children to conventional school.

The National Curriculum outlines minimum requirements and at WES we are able to offer a much broader framework, linking areas thematically whenever feasible. In the home setting there are fewer constraints on time as parents do not have to cope with thirty or more pupils, all with their different requirements. Parents can therefore, cover the same material as would be taught in school, in less time. In addition, they will be able to develop subjects, following their own child's interests. Moreover, home school parents are in the best position to assess the individual needs of their child and to plan work accordingly. They will find that they can become more easily involved in practical activities and to link learning with the real world.

The home school situation allows parents the choice of following the WES curriculum as freely or as closely as they wish. A word that parents often use when talking about our Home School Courses is flexibility, i.e. the freedom to begin the courses whenever they like and to organise their time to suit their own circumstances. They also appreciate the fact that the whole family can become part of the educational process.

Below is a typical comment from a Home School family:

"We really enjoy the freedom of home-school - being in control of how, when and where the teaching takes place instead of being restricted to school timetables and limitations."

The World-wide Education Service has its roots in the Parents' National Educational Union (P.N.E.U.), a non profit-making educational charity which was established by the educational pioneer, Charlotte Mason. Since 1990 WES has joined with the Bell Educational Trust (BET). BET is also a non profit-making organisation which specialises in the teaching of English as a foreign language.

For further information, please contact:

The Home School Service
World-wide Education Service of the Bell Educational Trust,
10 Barley Mow Passage
Chiswick
London W4 4PH

Telephone: 0181 994 3622   Fax: 0181 747 8376

Useful Addresses

Education Otherwise
P.O.Box 7420, London N9 9SG

telephone helpline 0891 518303
(This is a support group for home educating families)

Home Education Advisory Service
P.O.Box 98, Welwyn Garden City, Herts AL8 6AN
(This is an advice group for home educating families)

Education Now Publishing Co-operative Ltd.,
113 Arundel Drive, Bramcote Hills, Nottingham NG9 3FQ
(This is a non-profit making research, writing and publishing co-operative
devoted to the development of more flexible forms of education)

The Home school Service
World-wide Education Service of the Bell Educational Trust,
10 Barley Mow Passage
Chiswick
London W4 4PH

Telephone: 0181 994 3622   Fax: 0181 747 8376

Reading and References

John Holt *Teach Your Own* Lighthouse Books ISBN 0 907637 00 0

Roland Meighan *The Next Learning System: and why home-schoolers are
trailblazers* Educational Heretics Press ISBN 1-900219-04-2

Alice Miller *For Your Own Good: The Roots of Violence in Child-rearing*
Virago ISBN 0 86068 899 2

Julie Webb *Children Learning At Home* Falmer Press ISBN 1 85000 812 4

(a longer list of books and journal articles can be obtained from Education
Now)

EDUCATION NOW

Aim: *Education Now* is an organisation that is concerned to help develop arrangements for learning that will be flexible enough to provide **'alternatives for everybody, all the time'**. It supports individuals and initiatives that try to make the best out of the present system as we work for a better learning system.

Justification: The present education system, based on a factory model of mass schooling, is now coming to be seen as more and more obsolete. In a rapidly changing world, with its information-rich environment and new communication technologies, and its new research on how the brain works, the case for traditional schooling gets weaker by the year. By contrast, the case for an education that will give people resourcefulness, flexibility, confidence in learning lifelong, readiness to unlearn redundant ideas, grows ever stronger.

Those associated with *Education Now* share a commitment to the values which are set out in its *Statement of Purpose*. All the activities of the organisation are designed to promote the key ideas of flexibility, diversity, co-operation, democracy, self-motivation, learner-choice and responsibility, equal opportunity and personalisation of learning both in and out of state-provided education.   Our key book is *Flexi-schooling: Education for Tomorrow, Starting Yesterday*.

Status: Education Now Ltd is a research, writing, consultancy and publishing group, working as a co-operative. It is a company limited by guarantee, is registered for VAT, and is authorised to use a charity number, as a not-for-profit organisation.

EDUCATION NOW maintains that people learn best:

- when they are self-motivated
- when they take responsibility for their own lives and learning
- when they feel comfortable in their surroundings
- when teachers and learners value, trust, respect and listen to each other
- when education is seen as a life-long process

EDUCATION NOW PUBLICATIONS

News and Review: the quarterly publication which promotes the vision and ideas of *Education Now*

....

Information Packs: on *Home-based Education,* on *Flexi-time Schooling,* and on *The Next Learning System to replace Mass Schooling*

....

Books: ***Developing Democratic Education*** edited by Clive Harber £9-95
Democracy is not genetic - it is learned behaviour, but schools are currently organised on anti-democratic principles.

Early Childhood Education: The Way Forward
edited by Philip Gammage and Janet Meighan £9-95
This is essential reading for all involved in the education of young children.

Learning Technology, Science and Social Justice: an integrated approach for 3-13 year olds by John Siraj-Blatchford £13-95

Beyond Authoritarian School Management by Lynn Davies £9-95
...vital reading for anyone keen to move beyond the limitations of authoritarian school management into more effective forms of practice

Sharing Power in Schools: Raising Standards by Bernard Trafford £4-95
... our students are becoming more effective, self-confident and imaginative learners and workers. Examination results are improving ...

Never Too Late by John Holt £9-95
I applaud this book heartily ... Sir Yehudi Menuhin

Learning From Home-based Education edited by Roland Meighan £4-95
...the rich diversity of the home-based phenomenon is demonstrated.

Praxis Makes Perfect: Critical Educational Research for Social Justice
by Iram Siraj-Blatchford £6-95
The author is a black feminist who has long been concerned with the question of whose knowledge and intellectual frames are represented by the academy.

The Further Education Curriculum by Anna Frankel & Frank Reeves £9-50
The Modernity of Further Education by Frank Reeves £9-50
Further Education and Democracy by Keith Wymer £9-50

Full list from: **Education Now, 113 Arundel Drive, Bramcote Hills, Nottingham NG9 3FQ** Tel/fax 0115 925 7261